Wetlands

Quinn M. Arnold

seedlings

CREATIVE EDUCATION • CREATIVE PAPERBACKS

Published by Creative Education and Creative Paperbacks
P.O. Box 227, Mankato, Minnesota 56002
Creative Education and Creative Paperbacks
are imprints of The Creative Company
www.thecreativecompany.us

Design by Ellen Huber; production by Joe Kahnke
Art direction by Rita Marshall
Printed in the United States of America

Photographs by Alamy (Radius Images), Dreamstime (9comeback,
Baloncici, Tony Campbell, Ryan Carter, Derkien, Edwardje,
Jimmytst, Andrew Kazmierski, Kenneth Keifer, Kingan,
Aliaksandr Mazurkevich, Greg Mcgill, Nika111, Pbclub, Scott
Sanders, Diamantis Seitanidis, Sommai Sommai, Xiaomin Wang,
Thomas Waters), iStockphoto (CreativeNature_nl, egal, salajean),
Shutterstock (Nazeri Mamat)

Library of Congress Cataloging-in-Publication Data
Arnold, Quinn M.
Wetlands / Quinn M. Arnold.
p. cm. — (Seedlings)
Includes bibliographical references and index.
Summary: A kindergarten-level introduction to wetlands,
covering their climate, plant and animal life, and such
defining features as their shallow waters.
ISBN 978-1-60818-798-0 (hardcover)
ISBN 978-1-62832-351-1 (pbk)
ISBN 978-1-56660-845-9 (eBook)
1. Wetlands—Juvenile literature.
QH541.5.M3 A76 2016
577.68—dc23   2015041995
CCSS: RI.K.1, 2, 3, 4, 5, 6, 7;
RI.1.1, 2, 3, 4, 5, 6, 7; RF.K.1, 3; RF.1.1

First Edition HC 9 8 7 6 5 4 3 2 1
First Edition PBK 9 8 7 6 5 4 3 2 1

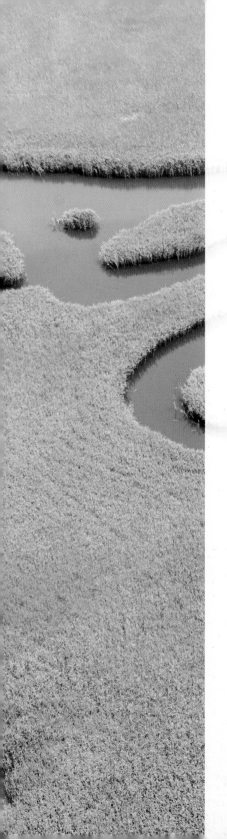

TABLE OF CONTENTS

Hello, wetland!

Wetlands are large, damp areas.

Some have salty
water. Others
have fresh water.

Many plants and animals live in wetlands. Moss grows on trees.

Great blue herons wade in shallow waters.

Salty wetlands have mangrove trees.

Crocodiles lie still in the sun. Fish swim in the warm water.

Tall cattails grow in freshwater wetlands. Frogs leap onto lily pads.

They look for bugs to eat.

13

Wetlands are found in many places on Earth. Some are always covered with water. Others flood each year.

Plants grow in wet soil.
Birds watch for food.

Turtles hide in their shells.

Goodbye, wetland!

Picture a Wetland

marsh

grass

water lilies

lily pad

frog

swamp

cypress tree

Spanish moss

alligator

water

21

damp: slightly wet; damp ground is soft and mushy

wade: to walk through water; wading birds like herons have long legs

Read More

Dayton, Connor. *Wetland Animals.*
New York: PowerKids Press, 2009.

Heos, Bridget. *Do You Really Want to Visit a Wetland?*
Mankato, Minn.: Amicus, 2015.

Websites

DragonflyTV: Wetlands
http://pbskids.org/dragonflytv/show/wetlands.html
Watch a video to learn more about different kinds
of wetlands.

What Is a Wetland?
http://www.nwf.org/Kids/Ranger-Rick/Animals/Mixture-of
-Species/What-Is-A-Wetland.aspx
Discover more about wetlands with Wet Wally the frog.

Index

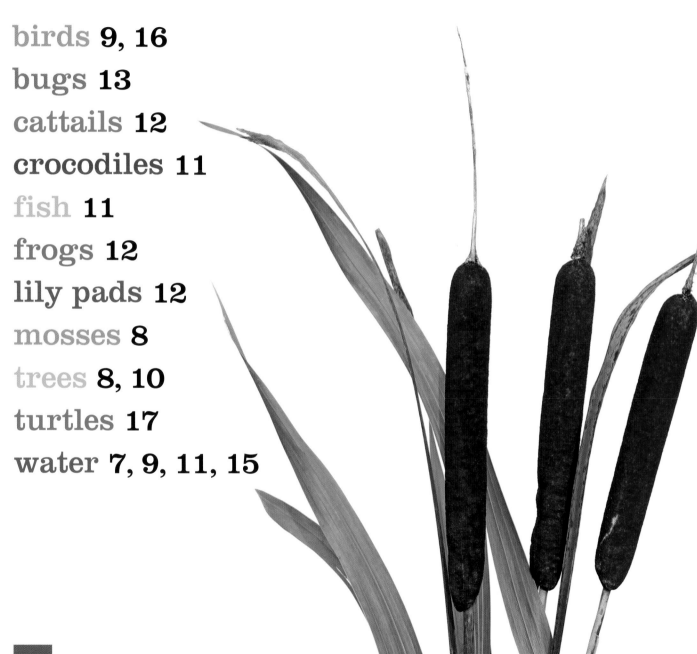